Together, We Are FIERCE

By Jenny Dearinger
Inspired By Juanetta White

Copyright 2022 by Jenny Dearinger

All rights reserved. No part of this publication including pictures may be reproduced, stored in a retrieval system, of transmitted in any form or by any means, electronic, mechanical, recording or otherwise, without prior written permission of the author. This book is for entertainment purposes only. The views expressed are by the authors alone.

Dedication

I would like to thank the person who inspired this story, Juanetta White. As a Life Coach, Juanetta seeks to energize and motivate. She has certainly empowered me to help children understand that their future is not predetermined, that they have the power to not only be successful individuals, but by working together, they can change the world. Thank you, Mrs. White.

Unity is strength…
When there is teamwork and collaboration, wonderful things can be achieved.

— Mattie Stepanek

When I am alone, I am master
Of my world.
I am smart.
I am confident.
I am worthy.

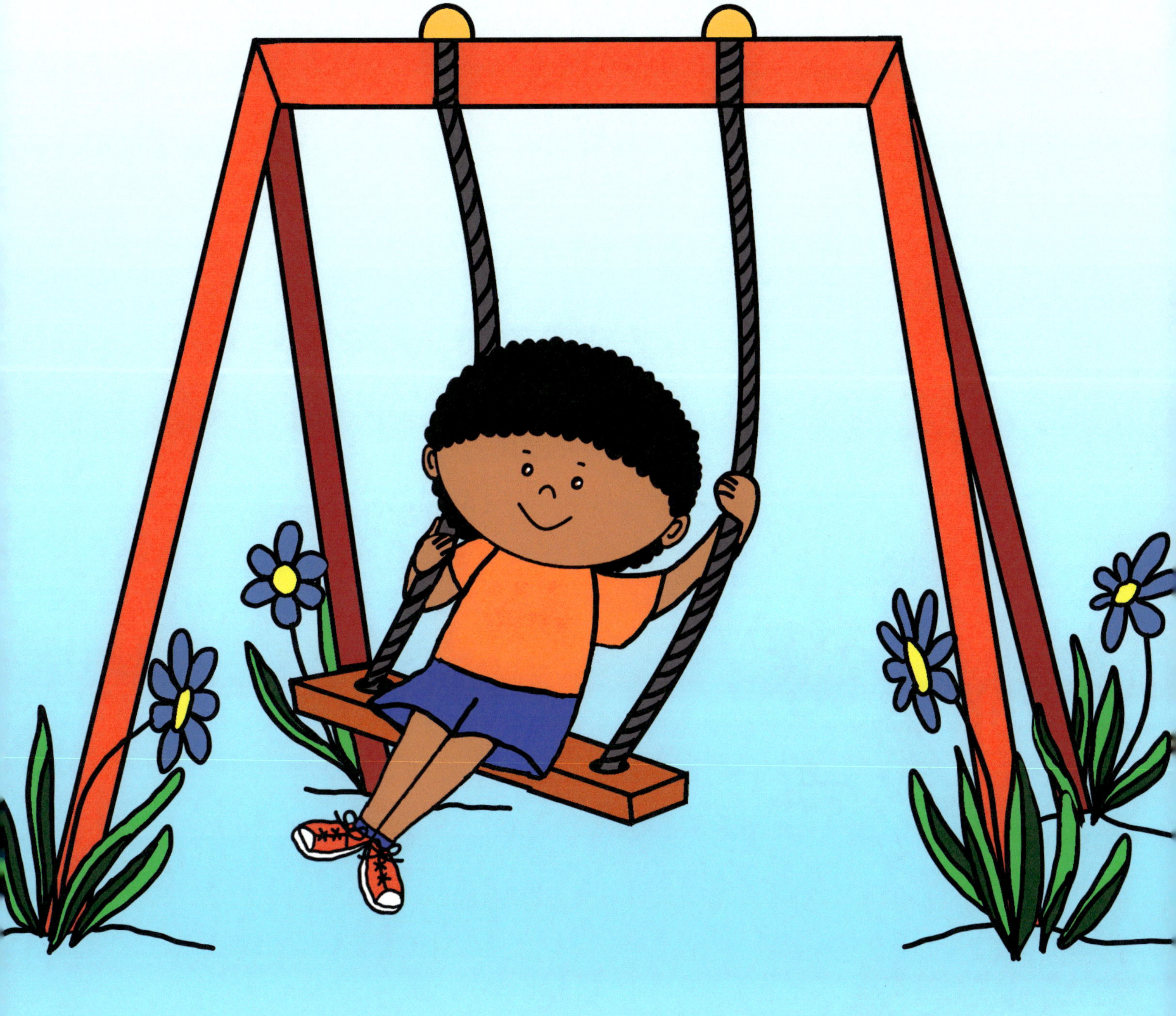

My voice matters.

My presence matters.

Nothing and nobody can

Change the fact

That I matter.

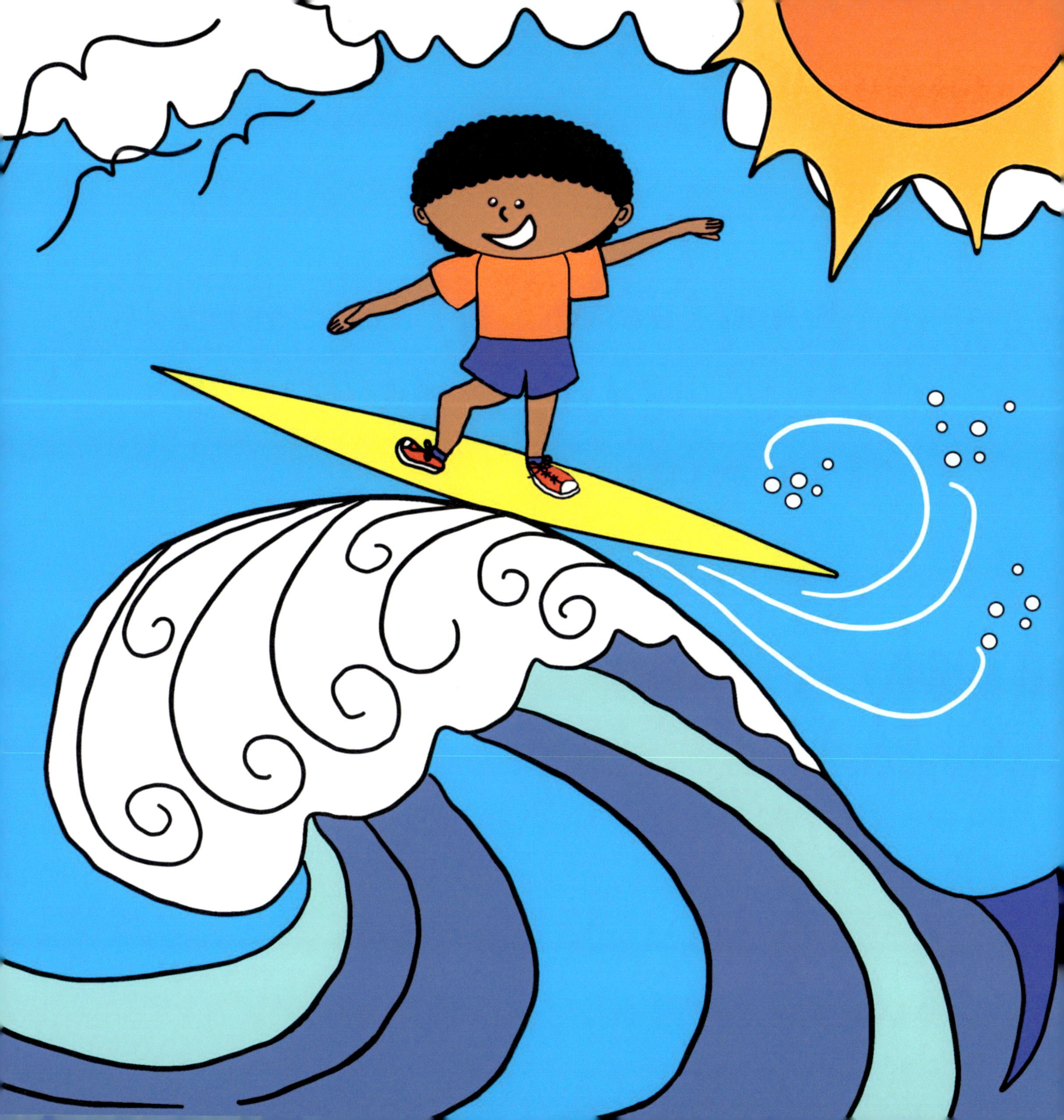

When I am alone, I am master
Of my world.

I am smart.

I am confident.

I am worthy.

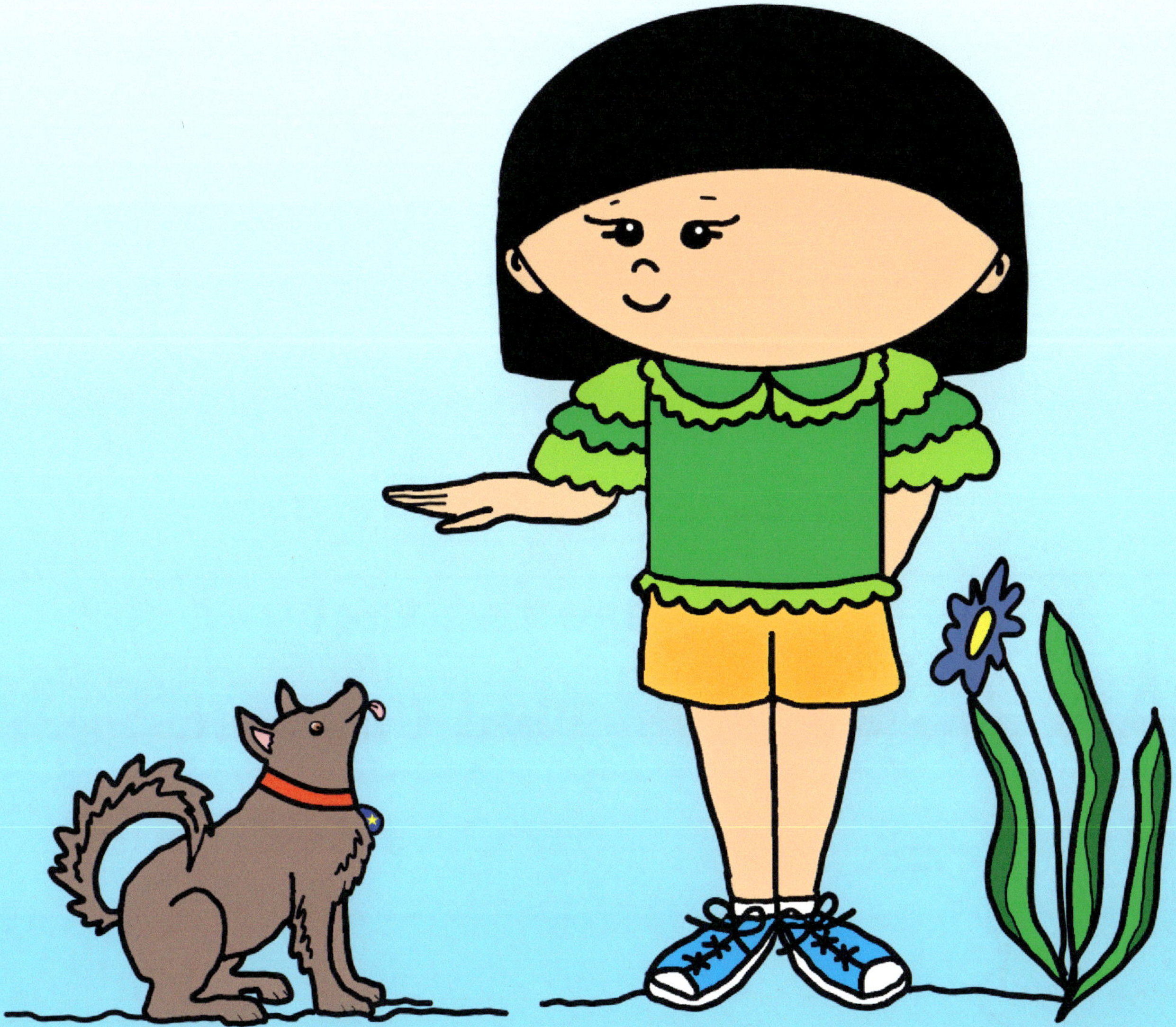

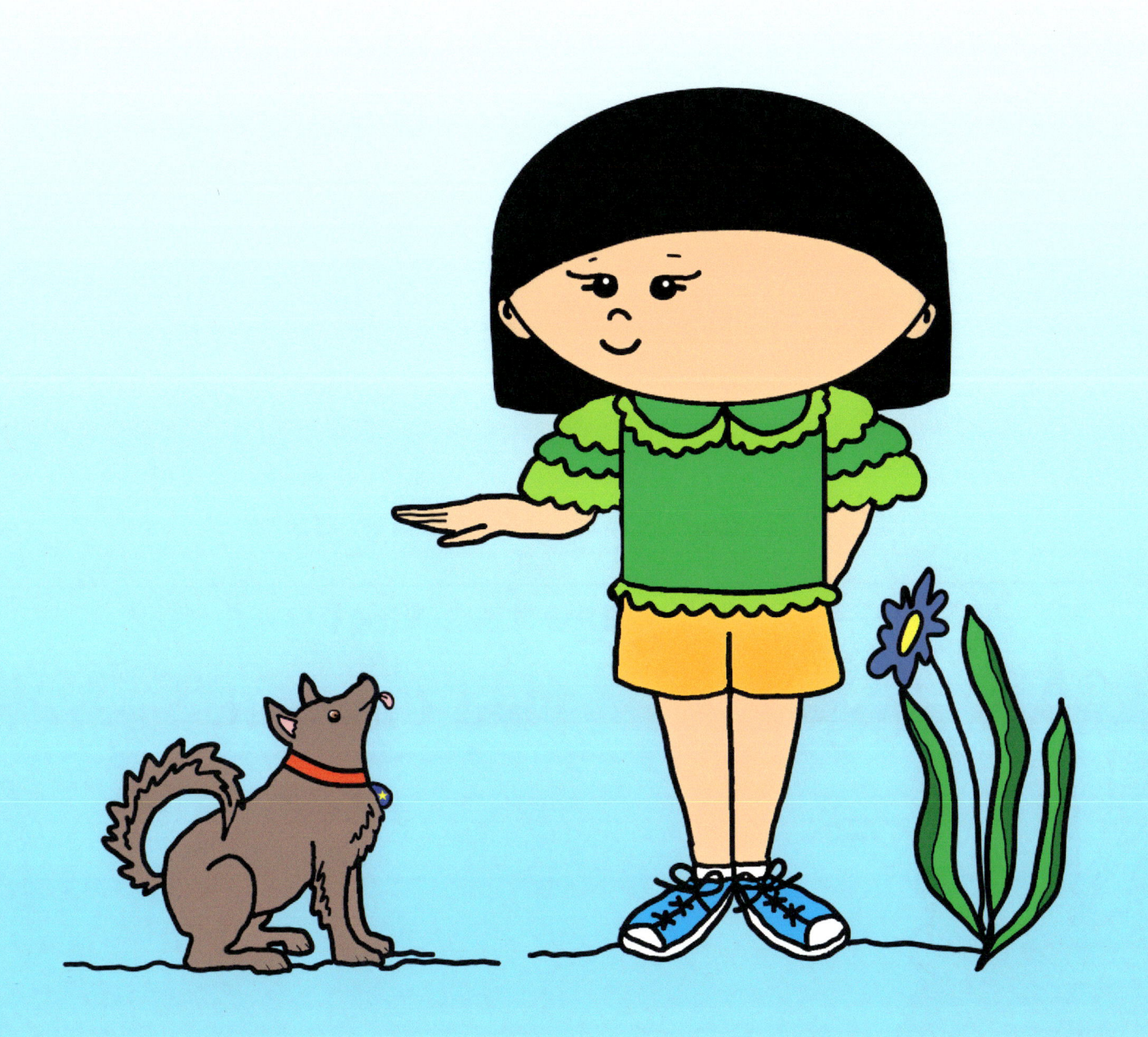

My voice matters.

My presence matters.

Nothing and nobody can

Change the fact

That I matter.

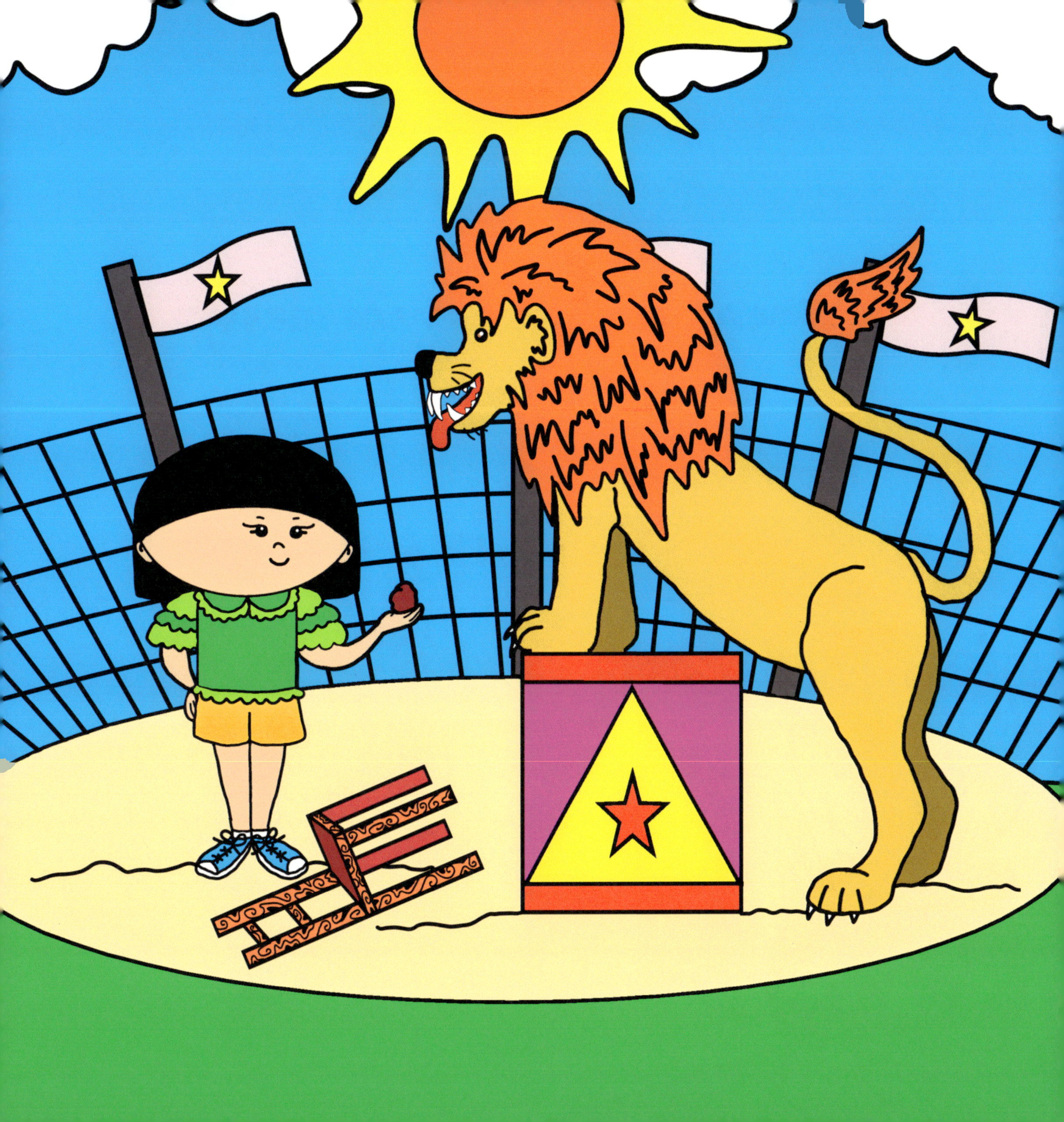

When I am alone, I am master
Of my world.
I am smart.
I am confident.
I am worthy.

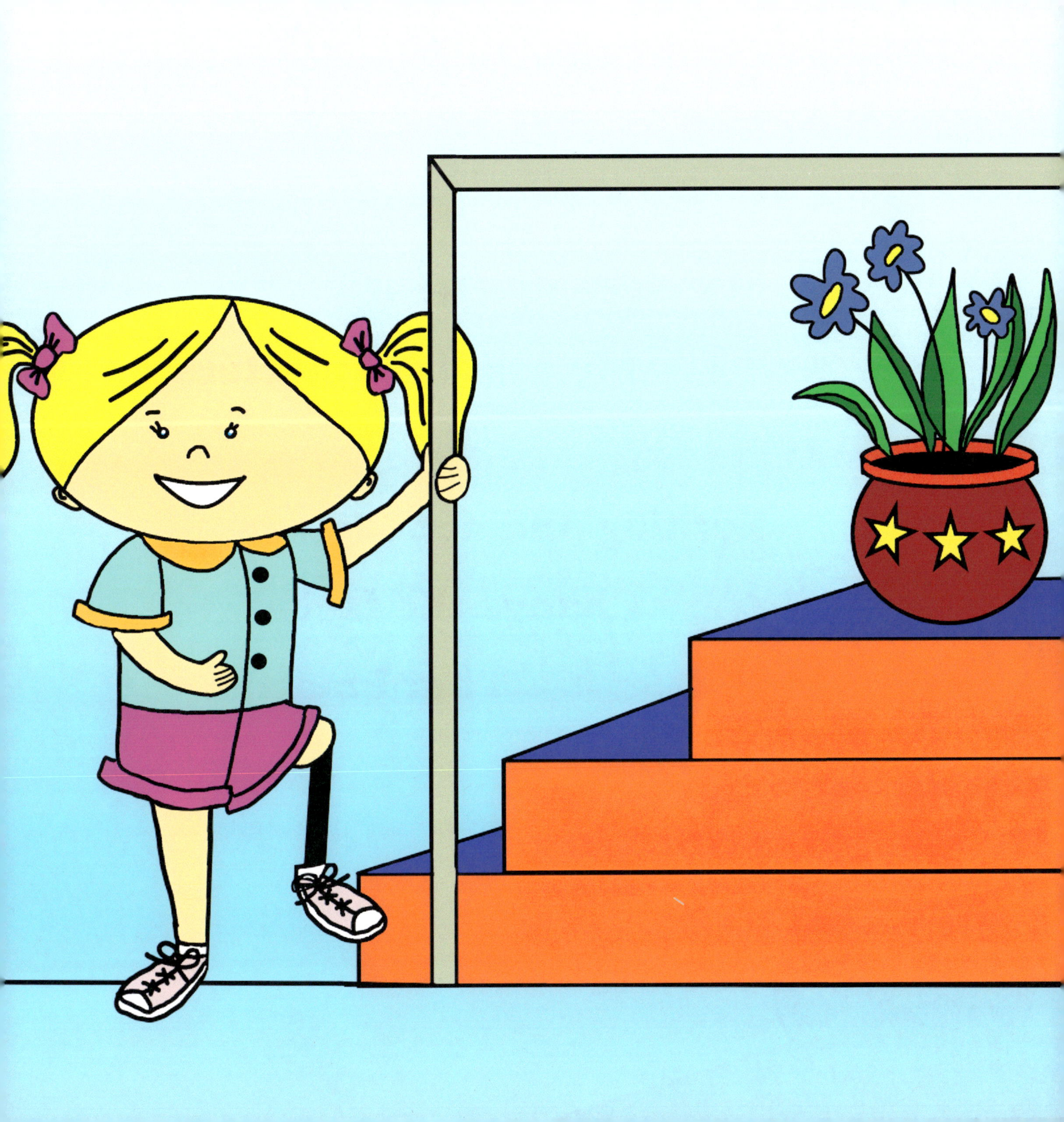

My voice matters.

      My presence matters.

Nothing and nobody can

      Change the fact

           That I matter.

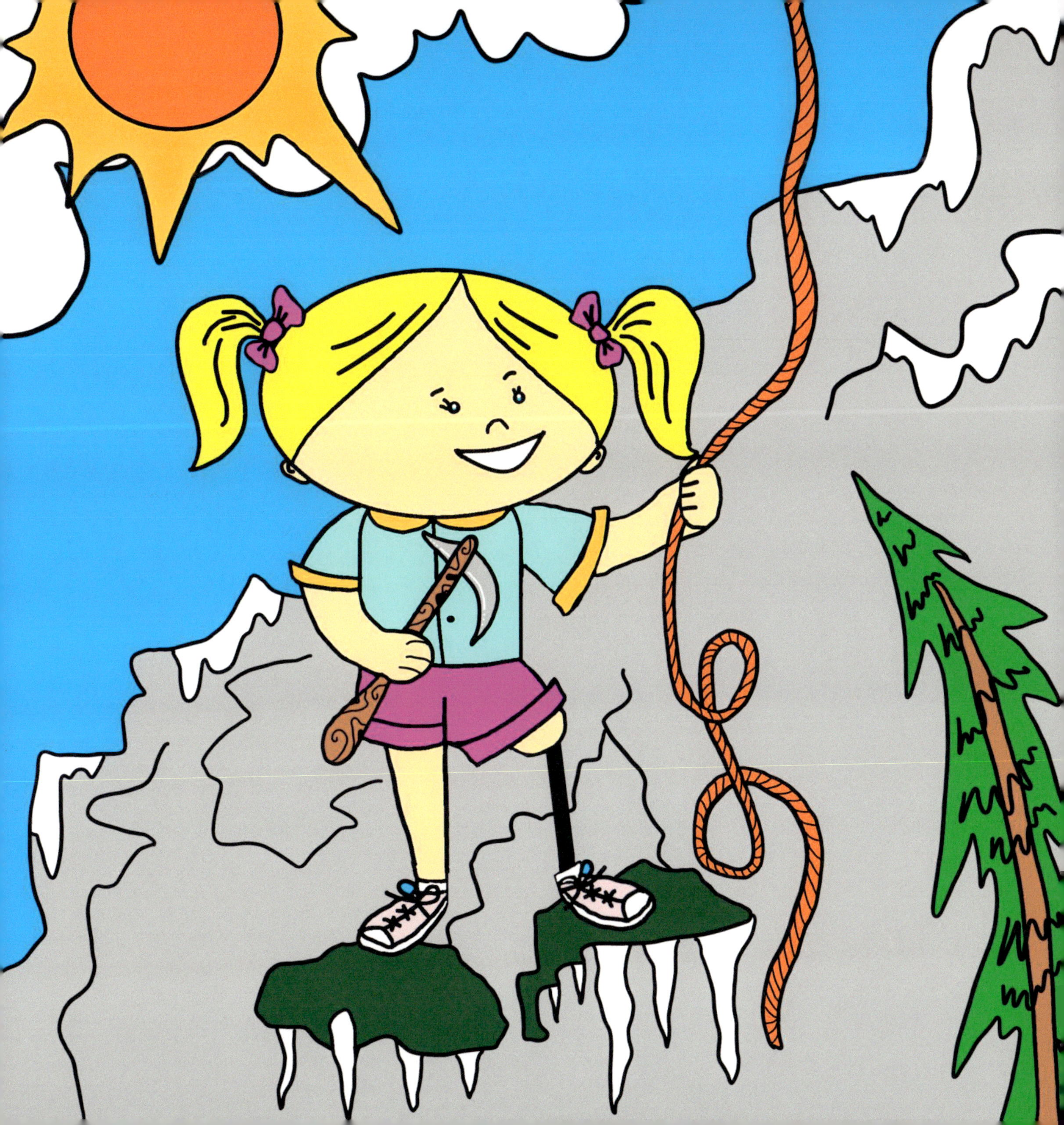

But.....

When I am with you,

　　　WE are masters of the

UNIVERSE!

We are smart.

　　　We are clever.

　　　　　We are worthy.

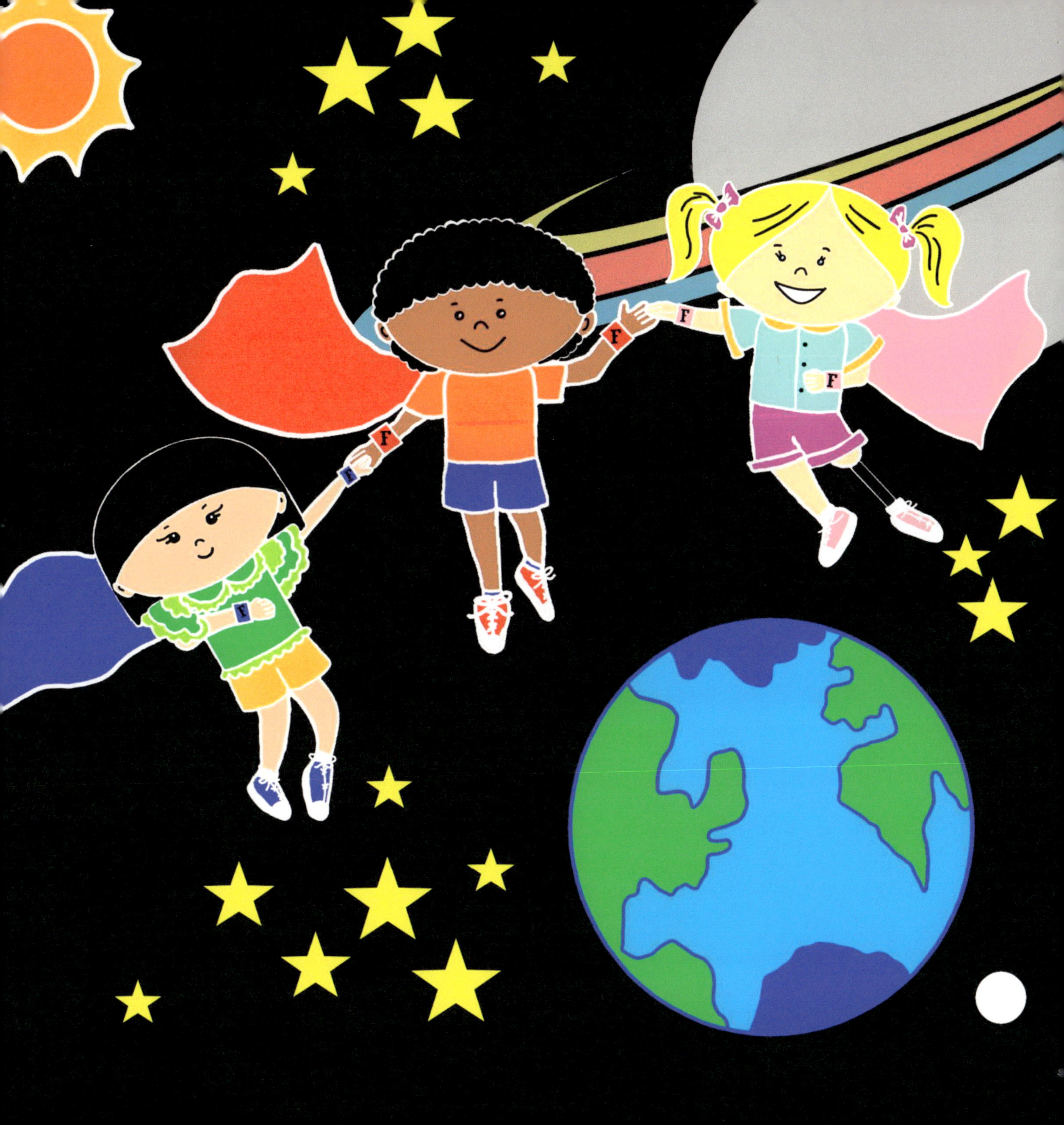

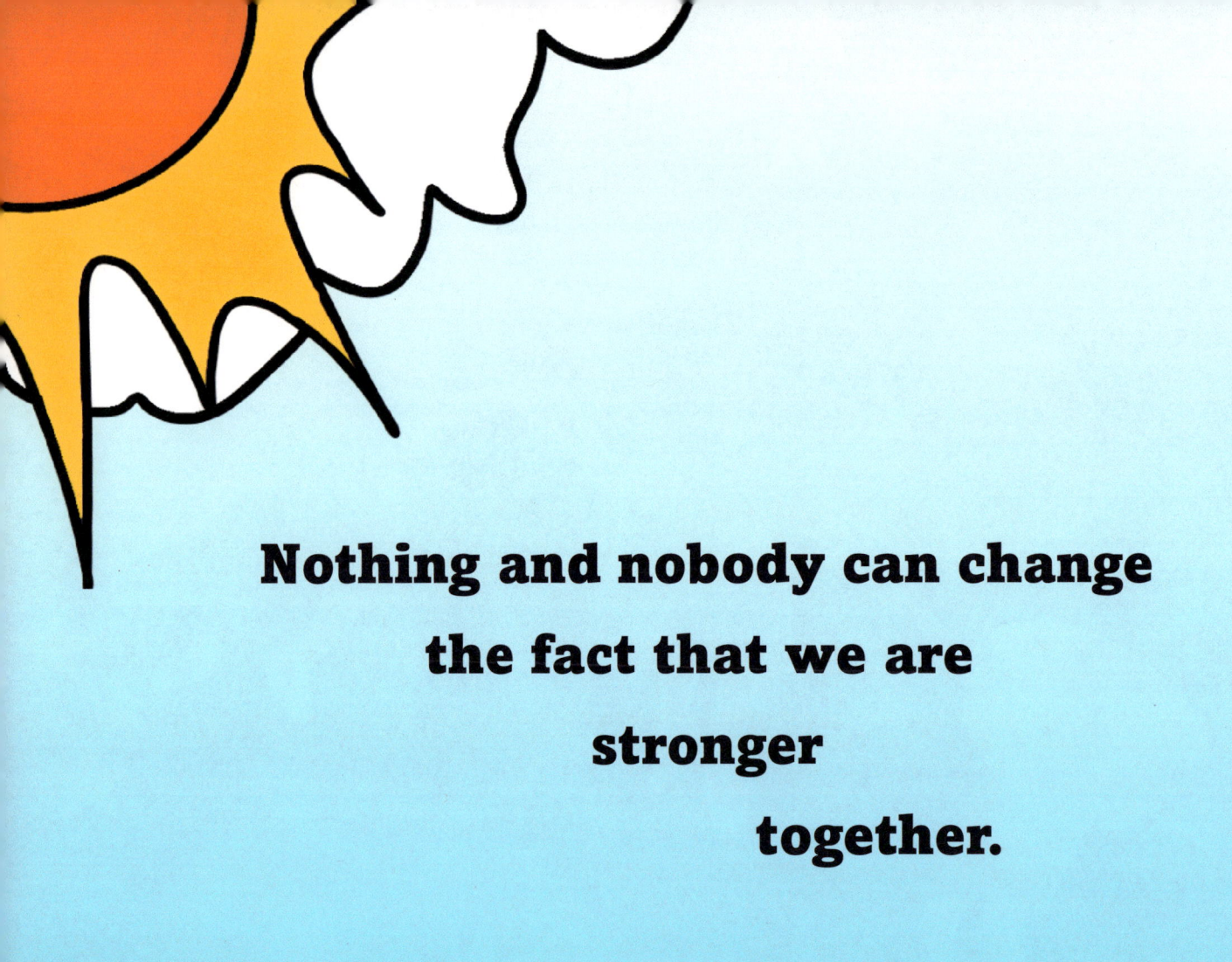

**Nothing and nobody can change
the fact that we are
stronger
together.**

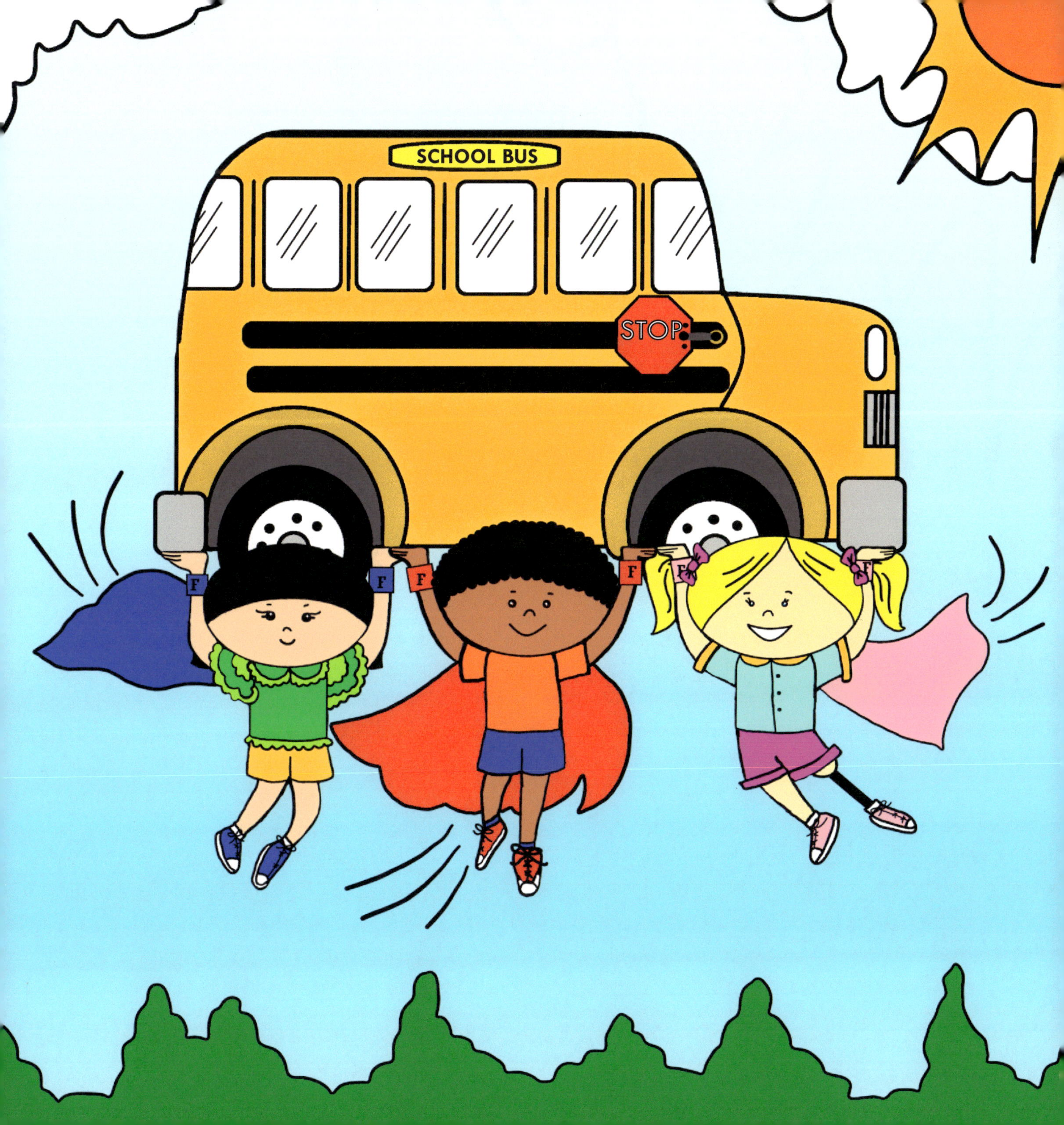
SCHOOL BUS
STOP

Together,
> Our voices rise above.

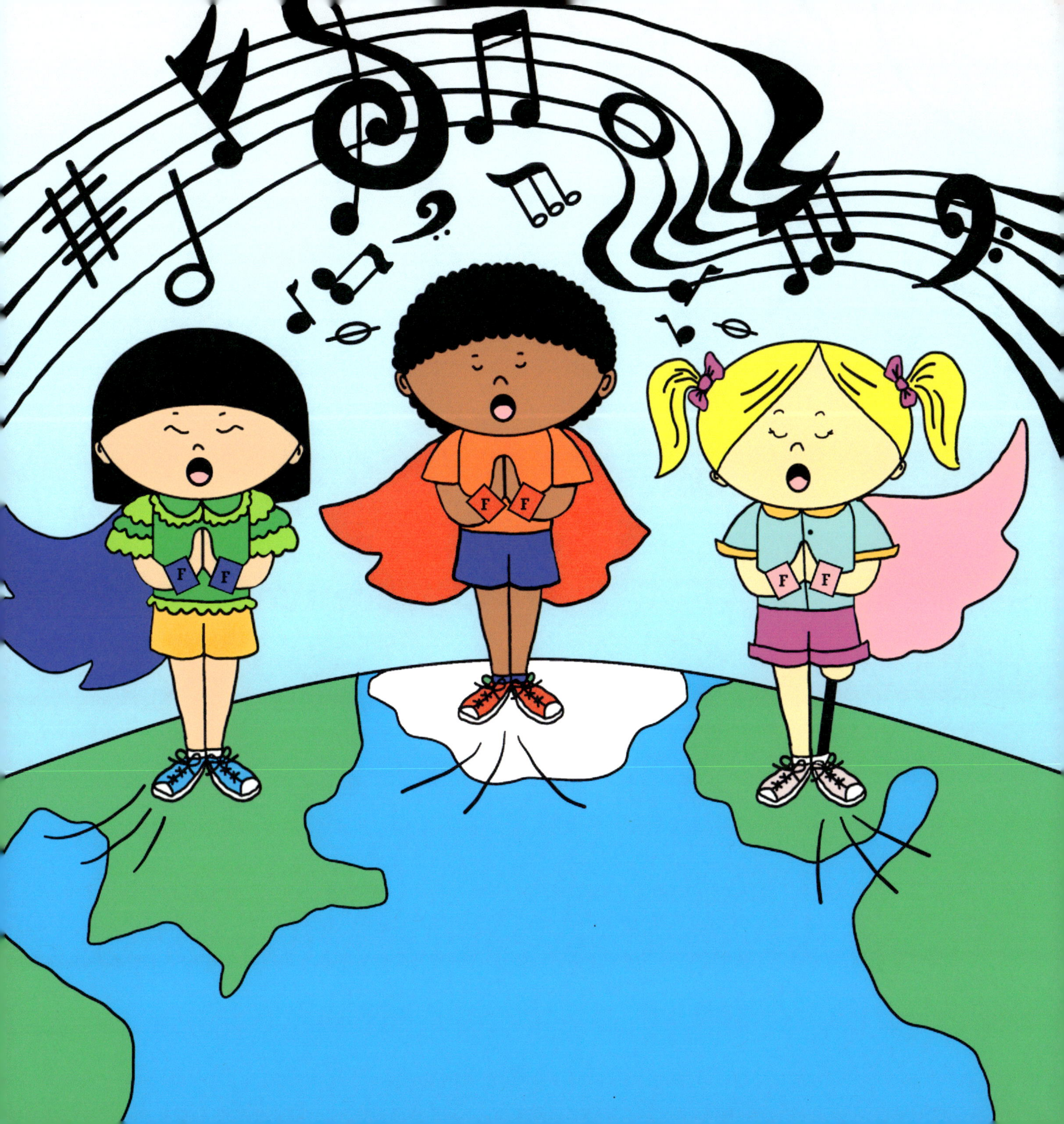

Together,
  We can make a
        Difference.

Together, We are *FIERCE.*

Made in the USA
Columbia, SC
28 November 2023